THE AMERICAN READER

A Brief Guide to
the Declaration of Independence,
the Constitution of the United States,
and the Bill of Rights

WORTH BOOKS
SMART SUMMARIES

Summary and analysis copyright © 2017 by Open Road Integrated Media, Inc.

ISBN: 978-1-5040-4865-1

Worth Books
180 Maiden Lane
New York, NY 10038
www.worthbooks.com

WORTH BOOKS
SMART SUMMARIES

Worth Books is a division of Open Road Integrated Media, Inc.

Contents

Introduction

The Declaration of Independence, the Constitution of the United States, and the Bill of Rights are the three most significant and seminal documents in American history.

The Declaration and the Constitution were drafted by the Second Continental Congress and the Constitutional Convention that met in the Independence Hall in Philadelphia in 1776 and 1787, respectively. The Bill of Rights, namely the first ten amendments to the Constitution, was proposed during one of the early sessions of the US Congress, which met in Federal Hall in New York City in 1789. Thomas Jefferson was the principal author of the Declaration of Independence while James Madison was the primary author of the Bill of Rights. Madison, along with Gouverneur Morris and James Wilson, also helped shape the Constitution.

The foundation of all three documents is the belief that all people have certain basic—or, inalienable—rights and that the government is responsible for protecting them. These rights encompass common law rights—the concept of which originates from English acts and laws like the Magna Carta and the 1689 Bill of Rights—and natural rights—which, the Founding Fathers believed, belong inherently to all by virtue of their humanity; no legitimate government may change or violate them.

Despite the unifying purpose of preserving the rights of the people, the Declaration of Independence and the Constitution, and therefore, the Bill of Rights, each serve different functions. The Declaration was written to justify America's breaking away from England's sovereignty, while the Constitution was designed to establish an entirely new government. The Declaration served its purpose—America gained independence from England on July 4, 1776—and has never been revised. On the other hand, the Constitution—which adapts to the needs of the people—has been amended twenty-seven times. The document allows for a functional, flexible, and responsive governing body, empowered to preserve the blessings of liberty for "We the People of the United States." The first ten amendments of the Constitution, however, remain unaltered, and speak to the colonists' fear of an overly centralized government. In this sense, the Constitution and its Bill of Rights complement the Declaration by proving America's ability to govern its people and defend personal liberties.

These documents are the foundation of our federal republic, and they represent what is best about the US system of government. They are symbols of the liberty that continues to attract people from all over the world to the United States, promoting that all are equal in the eyes of the law.

In the centuries since the creation of our founding documents, the liberties set forth within them have faced many challenges—including war, unrest, political debate, and legal disputes. Those tests persist today, but the initial strength of these documents continues to withstand the test of time, shining as beacons of hope and freedom.

Timeline

February 10, 1763: The Treaty of Paris (also known as the Treaty of 1763) ends the French and Indian War, and France surrenders all of their North American possessions east of the Mississippi to Britain. While the treaty ended the war, the debts incurred and the cost of maintaining order in the acquired territory cause the British government to impose new taxes on the colonies.

March 22, 1765: The Stamp Act is passed by the British Parliament, taxing colonists for printed paper, including legal documents, licenses, newspapers, and even playing cards. The colonists rebel and success-fully repeal the Stamp Act the following year.

June 15 – July 2, 1767: Parliament passes the Townshend Acts, a series of four acts imposing taxes on lead, glass, paper, paint, and tea.

October 1768: British troops arrive in Boston to enforce the Townshend duties and suppress local radicals. The colonists refuse to accept the presence of the troops, leading to fights in the streets.

March 5, 1770: The Boston Massacre occurs when a local crowd begins harassing a group of British soldiers outside a customs house. The militiamen open fire, killing five civilians.

December 16, 1773: American patriots disguised as Mohawk Indians dump 342 chests of East India Company tea—valued at approximately $18,000 at the time—into Boston Harbor.

May–June 1774: The Coercive, or Intolerable Acts, strip Massachusetts of self-government and judicial independence, sparking a boycott of all British goods.

September 5–October 26, 1774: Colonial delegates meet at the First Continental Congress to organize opposition to the Intolerable Acts.

April 19, 1775: The battles of Lexington and Concord are the first engagements between British soldiers and the armed civilian colonists who become known as Minutemen.

December 22, 1775: Parliament passes the Prohibitory Act, which establishes a blockade of US ports and declares American ships to be enemy vessels.

January 9, 1776: Thomas Paine's *Common Sense* is published anonymously.

July 4, 1776: The Second Continental Congress adopts the Declaration of Independence.

February 6, 1778: France recognizes the United States of America as an independent nation.

March 1, 1781: The Articles of Confederation are ratified by all thirteen states.

October 18, 1781: British forces surrender in Yorktown, Virginia.

March 5, 1782: The British Parliament votes to authorize peace negotiations.

September 3, 1783: The Treaty of Paris formally ends the Revolutionary War, recognizes American independence, and establishes US borders.

1786–1787: Continental Army Captain Daniel Shays leads a violent uprising against debt collection in Massachusetts that comes to be known as Shays' Rebellion.

May 25, 1787: The Constitutional Convention begins in Philadelphia, and fifty-five delegates from every state, excluding Rhode Island, begin drafting the Constitution.

September 17, 1787: The Constitutional Convention ends with members signing the final draft of the Constitution.

June 21, 1788: New Hampshire ratifies the Constitution, the ninth state to do so, which allows the document to become the law of the land.

March 4, 1789: The new US government, under the Constitution, formally begins.

September 25, 1789: Congress proposes twelve amendments to the Constitution.

December 15, 1791: Congress ratifies ten of the twelve proposed amendments, which become the Bill of Rights.

The Declaration of Independence

In Congress, July 4, 1776.

The unanimous Declaration of the thirteen united States of America, When in the Course of human events, it becomes necessary for one people to dissolve the political bands which have connected them with another, and to assume among the powers of the earth, the separate and equal station to which the Laws of Nature and of Nature's God entitle them, a decent respect to the opinions of mankind requires that they should declare the causes which impel them to the separation.

We hold these truths to be self-evident, that all men are created equal, that they are endowed by their Creator with certain unalienable Rights, that among these are Life, Liberty and the pursuit of Happiness.— That to secure these rights, Governments are instituted among Men, deriving their just powers from the consent of the governed,— That whenever any Form of Government becomes destructive of these ends, it is the Right of the People to alter or to abolish it, and to institute new Government, laying its foundation on such principles and organizing its powers in such form, as to them shall seem most likely to effect their Safety and Happiness. Prudence, indeed, will dictate that Governments long established should not be changed for light and transient causes; and accordingly all experience hath shewn, that mankind are more disposed to suffer, while evils are sufferable, than to right themselves by abolishing the forms to which they are accustomed. But when a long train of abuses and usurpations, pursuing invariably the same Object evinces a design to reduce them under absolute Despotism, it is their right, it is their duty, to throw off such Government, and to provide new Guards for their future security.— Such has been the patient sufferance of these Colonies; and such is now the necessity which constrains them to alter their former Systems of Government. The history of the present King of Great Britain is a history of repeated injuries and usurpations, all having in direct object the establishment of an absolute Tyranny over these States. To prove this, let Facts be submitted to a candid world.

He has refused his Assent to Laws, the most wholesome and necessary for the public good.

He has forbidden his Governors to pass Laws of immediate and pressing importance, unless suspended in their operation till his Assent should be obtained; and when so suspended, he has utterly neglected to attend to them.

He has refused to pass other Laws for the accommodation of large districts of people, unless those people would relinquish the right of Representation in the Legislature, a right inestimable to them and formidable to tyrants only.

He has called together legislative bodies at places unusual, uncomfortable, and distant from the depository of their public Records, for the sole purpose of fatiguing them into compliance with his measures.

He has dissolved Representative Houses repeatedly, for opposing with manly firmness his invasions on the rights of the people.

He has refused for a long time, after such dissolutions, to cause others to be elected; whereby the Legislative powers, incapable of Annihilation, have returned to the People at large for their exercise; the State remaining in the mean time exposed to all the dangers of invasion from without, and convulsions within.

He has endeavoured to prevent the population of these States; for that purpose obstructing the Laws for Naturalization of Foreigners; refusing to pass others to encourage their migrations hither, and raising the conditions of new Appropriations of Lands.

He has obstructed the Administration of Justice, by refusing his Assent to Laws for establishing Judiciary powers.

He has made Judges dependent on his Will alone, for the tenure of their offices, and the amount and payment of their salaries.

He has erected a multitude of New Offices, and sent hither swarms of Officers to harrass our people, and eat out their substance.

He has kept among us, in times of peace, Standing Armies without the Consent of our legislatures.

He has affected to render the Military independent of and superior to the Civil power.

He has combined with others to subject us to a jurisdiction foreign to our constitution, and unacknowledged by our laws; giving his Assent to their Acts of pretended Legislation:

For Quartering large bodies of armed troops among us:

For protecting them, by a mock Trial, from punishment for any Murders which they should commit on the Inhabitants of these States:

For cutting off our Trade with all parts of the world:

For imposing Taxes on us without our Consent:

For depriving us in many cases, of the benefits of Trial by Jury:

For transporting us beyond Seas to be tried for pretended offences

For abolishing the free System of English Laws in a neighbouring Province, establishing therein an Arbitrary government, and enlarging its Boundaries so as to render it at once an example and fit instrument for introducing the same absolute rule into these Colonies:

For taking away our Charters, abolishing our most valuable Laws, and altering fundamentally the Forms of our Governments:

For suspending our own Legislatures, and declaring themselves invested with power to legislate for us in all cases whatsoever.

He has abdicated Government here, by declaring us out of his Protection and waging War against us.

He has plundered our seas, ravaged our Coasts, burnt our towns, and destroyed the lives of our people.

He is at this time transporting large Armies of foreign Mercenaries to compleat the works of death, desolation and tyranny, already begun with circumstances of Cruelty & perfidy scarcely paralleled in the most barbarous ages, and totally unworthy the Head of a civilized nation.

He has constrained our fellow Citizens taken Captive on the high Seas to bear Arms against their Country, to become the executioners of their friends and Brethren, or to fall themselves by their Hands.

He has excited domestic insurrections amongst us, and has endeavoured to bring on the inhabitants of our frontiers, the merciless Indian Savages, whose known rule of warfare, is an undistinguished destruction of all ages, sexes and conditions.

In every stage of these Oppressions We have Petitioned for Redress in the most humble terms: Our repeated Petitions have been answered only by repeated injury. A Prince whose character is thus marked by every act which may define a Tyrant, is unfit to be the ruler of a free people.

Nor have We been wanting in attentions to our British brethren. We have warned them from time to time of attempts by their legislature to extend an unwarrantable jurisdiction over us. We have reminded them of the circumstances of our emigration and settlement here. We have appealed to their native justice and magnanimity, and we have conjured them by the ties of our common kindred to disavow these usurpations, which, would inevitably interrupt our connections and correspondence. They too have been deaf to the voice of justice and of consanguinity. We must, therefore, acquiesce in the necessity, which denounces our Separation, and hold them, as we hold the rest of mankind, Enemies in War, in Peace Friends.

We, therefore, the Representatives of the united States of America, in General Congress, Assembled, appealing to the Supreme Judge of the world for the rectitude of our intentions, do, in the Name, and by Authority of the good People of these Colonies, solemnly publish and declare, That these United Colonies are, and of Right ought to be Free and Independent States; that they are Absolved from all Allegiance to the British Crown, and that all political connection between them and the State of Great Britain, is and ought to be totally dissolved; and that as Free and Independent States, they have full Power to levy War, conclude Peace, contract Alliances, establish Commerce, and to do all other Acts and Things which Independent States may of right do. And for the support of this Declaration, with a firm reliance on the protection of divine Providence, we mutually pledge to each other our Lives, our Fortunes and our sacred Honor.

Georgia
Button Gwinnett
Lyman Hall
George Walton

North Carolina
William Hooper
Joseph Hewes
John Penn

South Carolina
Edward Rutledge
Thomas Heyward, Jr.
Thomas Lynch, Jr.
Arthur Middleton

Massachusetts
John Hancock

Maryland
Samuel Chase
William Paca
Thomas Stone
Charles Carroll of Carrollton

New York
William Floyd
Philip Livingston
Francis Lewis
Lewis Morris

Virginia
George Wythe
Benjamin Harrison
Thomas Nelson, Jr.
Francis Lightfoot Lee
Carter Braxton

New Hampshire
Josiah Bartlett
William Whipple

Delaware
Caesar Rodney
George Read
Thomas McKean

New Jersey
Richard Stockton
John Witherspoon
Francis Hopkinson
John Hart
Abraham Clark

Massachusetts
Samuel Adams
John Adams
Robert Treat Paine
Elbridge Gerry

Rhode Island
Stephen Hopkins
William Ellery

New Hampshire
Matthew Thornton

Connecticut
Roger Sherman
Samuel Huntington
William Williams
Oliver Wolcott

Pennsylvania
Robert Morris
Benjamin Rush
Benjamin Franklin
John Morton
George Clymer
James Smith
George Taylor
James Wilson
George Ross

Context

Although we might view the adoption of the Declaration of Independence as inevitable, it was fairly unique in its time period. When the Declaration was issued in July 1776, the thirteen colonies and Great Britain had been at war for more than a year. The conflict dated back to Parliamentary measures to increase revenue from the colonies, such as the Stamp Act of 1765 and the Townshend Acts of 1767, which were viewed by the British as legitimate ways to make the colonies pay for their protection and maintenance. Many colonists, however, felt they were not directly represented in the government, and therefore, Parliament had no right to tax them.

British and American interpretations of the British Constitution and Parliament's authority over the colonies differed greatly. The British believed Parliament was the overall authority throughout the entire empire, so all of its actions were constitutional. The colonists, however, understood the British Constitution to recognize certain basic rights that no government could violate, not even Parliament. By 1774, Samuel Adams and Thomas Jefferson argued that Parliament represented Great Britain only, and the colonies, which had their own legislatures, were connected to the rest of the empire only by their allegiance to the Crown.

The crisis around authority in the colonies came to a head when Parliament passed the 1774 Coercive Acts, referred to by colonists as the Intolerable Acts, to punish Massachusetts for the Boston Tea Party. Many colonists saw the Coercive Acts as a violation of the British Constitution and, as such, a threat to the liberties of all of British America. In September 1774, the First Continental Congress met in Philadelphia to organize a response. They called for a boycott of British goods and petitioned the king for repeal of the acts. This did not achieve the desired effect. King George III and his prime minister were inflexible on the subject of Parliamentary supremacy. Colonists organized militias, gathered arms, and prepared to settle the issue in battle. Britain sent troops to seize the arms and arrest colonial leaders.

Still, most colonists still hoped to reconcile with

Great Britain, even after fighting began at Lexington and Concord in April 1775. The Second Continental Congress convened in Philadelphia that May. Some delegates wished for eventual independence, but no one wanted to declare it yet. Though most no longer believed Parliament had any sovereignty over the colonies, they still swore loyalty to King George, who they hoped would intervene on their behalf. They were disappointed in late 1775 when the king rejected Congress's second petition, issued a Proclamation of Rebellion, and announced on that he was recruiting foreign mercenaries to help suppress the uprising. A pro-American minority in Parliament warned the British government that it was driving the colonists toward independence.

In February 1776, colonists learned of Parliament's passing of the Prohibitory Act a few months prior. The act established a blockade of US ports and declared American ships to be enemy vessels. John Adams believed that Parliament had effectively declared American independence before the Second Continental Congress had drafted its proclamation. Public support for independence grew even stronger when it was confirmed that King George had obtained the support of German mercenaries for use against his American subjects.

The Second Continental Congress had no clear authority to declare independence. Delegates sent by thirteen different colonial governments were bound by the instructions given to them, which were not always in favor of succession. Public sentiment grew for separation from Great Britain, and advocates of independence sought to have the congressional instructions revised. Between April and July 1776, a complicated political battle was waged to bring this about.

In the campaign to revise congressional instructions, many American colonists formally expressed their support for separation from Great Britain in state and local declarations of independence. But the middle colonies of New York, New Jersey, Maryland, Pennsylvania, and Delaware still held back. In response, on May 10, the Second Continental Congress passed a resolution calling on undecided colonies to create new governments.

When approval had been received, the Second Continental Congress appointed a committee to draft a preamble to explain the purpose of the resolution. John Adams wrote the preamble, which was meant to encourage the overthrow of the governments of Pennsylvania and Maryland, both still under British proprietary governance. The preamble passed on May 15. Adams regarded this as America's declaration of independence, although a formal declaration would still have to be made.

On the same day, the Virginia Convention set the stage for a formal congressional declaration of independence by proposing to sever all bonds with Great Britain. Richard Henry Lee of Virginia presented a three-part resolution to the Second Continental Congress on June 7 to declare independence, form foreign alliances, and prepare a plan of colonial confederation. The motion was seconded by John Adams.

Lee's resolution was met with resistance, but support for a congressional declaration of independence was consolidated in the final weeks of June 1776. Connecticut, New Hampshire, and Delaware authorized their delegates to make such a declaration, and Pennsylvania dissolved its colonial assembly and established a new Conference of Committees, allowing their delegates to do the same. New Jersey arrested the royal governor, chose new representatives to the Second Continental Congress, and empowered them to join in a declaration. Maryland and New York had yet to recognize this authority in their delegrates, but Samuel Chase, with the help of local resolutions, was able to sway Maryland on June 28. Only the New York delegates were unable to get revised instructions.

Meanwhile, the Second Continental Congress needed an official document to explain the overall decision for independence. On June 11, 1776, it appointed a committee—consisting of John Adams, Benjamin Franklin, Thomas Jefferson, Robert R. Livingston, and Roger Sherman—to draft a declaration. Jefferson wrote the first draft. After consultation with the committee and alterations, a copy was presented to the Second Continental Congress on June 28, 1776. The title of the document was "A Declaration by the Representatives of the United States of America, in General Congress assembled."

For two days, the Second Continental Congress edited Jefferson's document, shortening it by a fourth, playing with the wording, and toying with the sentence structure. Among other things, in order to appease supporters of the Revolution in Britain, they took out Jefferson's claim that Britain forced slavery on the colonies.

On Monday, July 1, the Second Continental Congress set aside discussion of the declaration and resumed debate on Lee's resolution of independence. The next day, after a heated argument and some switches, back and forth, of allegiance, the resolution of independence was adopted with twelve affirmative votes and one abstention. And so, the colonies officially severed political ties with Great Britain.

After voting in favor of the resolution of independence, the Second Continental Congress again turned its attention to the committee's draft of the declaration. They made a few more changes but, on July 4, 1776, the wording of the Declaration of Independence was approved and sent to the printer for publication.

The United States of America officially declared itself a sovereign nation.

Analysis of Quotes from the Declaration of Independence

"When in the Course of human Events, it becomes necessary for one People to dissolve the political Bands which have connected them with another ... mankind requires that they should declare the causes which impel them to the separation."

The opening paragraph of the Declaration of Independence states one of its primary purposes, which is to explain the reasons for wanting separation from Great Britain. The Founding Fathers understood the importance of official recognition of their new nation by foreign powers and support from citizens of the world. It's also likely the Declaration was intended to persuade colonists, many of whom wished to remain under British rule.

"We, therefore, the Representatives of the united [sic] *States of America, in General Congress ... solemnly publish and declare, That these United Colonies are, and of Right ought to be Free and Independent States; that they are Absolved from all Allegiance to the British Crown."*

This directly states the purpose of the Declaration of Independence: to notify the world that the colonies are now free and independent states and, more importantly, "ought to be." In other words, that the claim to freedom from Britain is just, legal, and legitimate. This not only served to vindicate them in the eyes of more established nations, but also further garnered support from colonists who were on the fence or sympathized with Great Britain.

"Whenever any Form of Government becomes destructive of these ends, it is the Right of the People to alter or to abolish it, and to institute new Government, lay-

ing its foundation on such principles and organizing its powers in such form, as to them shall seem most likely to effect their Safety and Happiness."

This builds on John Locke's philosophy regarding the consent of the governed. If a ruler or government violates the trust of the people, it is the legal right of such people to rebel and replace that ruler or government. The implication (and later direct statement) is that King George III did just that, justifying the colonies' rebellion and separation. Further, the colonists had a rational plan to replace the tyrannical government with a representative and responsive one.

"Prudence, indeed, will dictate that Governments long established should not be changed for light and transient causes."

Separating from one's government is not done without grave cause, and the Founding Fathers wanted to emphasize that they were not wild-eyed revolutionaries, but men of law and reason who took this step out of necessity. Jefferson made sure to clearly state the colonies' awareness that declaring independence from the country that founded them required a very good reason. The Founding Fathers wanted very much to be seen as men of high purpose and good character.

"*A Prince whose character is thus marked by every act which may define a Tyrant, is unfit to be the ruler of a free people.*"

This gives insight into the Enlightenment view of both freedom and tyranny. Once again going back to Locke's philosophy of the consent of the governed, a free people (free by natural right), need not allow themselves to be governed by a ruler who acts arbitrarily. He, too, must submit to the rule of law. This is not only a basic right in the view of the Founding Fathers, but also a primary reason for declaring independence.

Analysis of Quotes About the Declaration of Independence

"We must be unanimous; there must be no pulling different ways; we must hang together." —John Hancock, July 4, 1776

In the process of signing the Declaration of Independence, the signatories made themselves opponents of the British Crown and army; in effect, they were committing treason. The verbiage of the Declaration itself seeks to explain why they felt this was not, in fact, sedition. Nevertheless, they were all aware that, should they lose the war, this act would be seen as criminal, and they would be tried and punished for it. Hancock's statement here identifies the need to stand together and stand strong in their beliefs in order to succeed.

"I have said that the Declaration of Independence is the ring-bolt to the chain of your nation's destiny; so, indeed, I regard it. The principles contained in that instrument are saving principles. Stand by those principles, be true to them on all occasions, in all places, against all foes, and at whatever cost."

—Frederick Douglass,
July 5, 1852

Using the imagery of a ring-bolt and chain—symbols of the slave trade—gives abolitionist Frederick Douglass's statement greater profundity. It would have been easy for Douglass, who escaped from slavery, to have written off the US government and the Declaration of Independence, as it did not free him from the threat of slavery. However, this quote, taken from his speech "What to a Slave is the Fourth of July?" is a call to remember that the principles set forth in the Declaration of Independence are inherently good and should, therefore, be protected against anyone meaning to dismantle them. He trusts that the foundational belief that all are created equal will eventually be the reason for the end of slavery in America.

"I am well aware of the Toil and Blood and Treasure, that it will cost Us to maintain this Declaration, and support and defend these States. Yet through all the Gloom I can see the Rays of ravishing Light and Glory. I can see that the End is more than worth all the Means. And that Posterity will tryumph in that Days Transaction, even altho We should rue it, which I trust in God We shall not." —John Adams to Abigail Adams, July 3, 1776

John Adams, who would become the nation's second president, writes to his wife in the midst of the creation of the Declaration of Independence. Here, he recognizes that the road to freedom is just beginning with this document and that there will be a price to pay for this choice—in other words, a full-blown war with England. Yet Adams looks beyond the devastation of battle to the life of freedom and self-rule that lies ahead if the United States is successful in separating from the Crown. Such a feat will be remembered throughout history, he feels, even if those involved now must pay a heavy price for it. The "glory" of creating this new nation will justify any difficulties required to get there.

"The Declaration, like Common Sense, was much more than a repudiation of George III. It put into words, even more effectively than Paine did, the principle which had been forming in the American mind, 'that all men are created equal.'"   —Edmund S. Morgan,
historian

When philosopher Thomas Paine's revolutionary pamplet *Common Sense* was being distributed throughout the colonies, a murmur began to rise among the people. They were dissatisfied with their ruler and wanted their voices to be heard. The Declaration of Independence took that murmur and made it impossible to ignore. The idea that "all men are created equal" seems obvious to us now, but at the time, it was a relatively new thought. If all are equal, why were the wants and needs of colonists ignored in favor of the needs of the Crown? The colonists believed that British rule should provide equal treatment for colonists and citizens alike.

"We find it hard to believe that liberty could ever be lost in this country. But it can be lost, and it will be, if the time ever comes when these documents are regarded not as the supreme expression of our profound belief, but merely as curiosities in glass cases."
—President Harry S. Truman,
December 15, 1952

Speaking at the National Archives, President Truman warns about the dangers of considering our founding documents to be merely historical papers. Instead, he says, the Declaration of Independence, the Constitution of the United States, and the Bill of Rights must continue to inspire awe in the citizens who have the privilege of gazing upon them. Not because they are important artifacts, but because the ideas contained therein are absolutely vital to the survival of our democracy. If we lose sight of the philosophy that "all men are created equal," for instance, we lose one of the foundational principles of our national identity.

Trivia

1. The Second Continental Congress officially declared its independence from Britain on July 2, 1776, but the final version of the Declaration of Independence was not approved until July 4, 1776, which is why we celebrate Independence Day on July 4.

2. Six people signed both the Declaration of Independence and the Constitution: George Clymer, Benjamin Franklin, Robert Morris, George Read, Roger Sherman, and James Wilson.

3. George Washington did not sign the Declaration of Independence even though he was a voting delegate from Virginia when the Second Continental Congress convened on May 10, 1775. Thirty-six days after convening, Washington was appointed commander in chief of the Continental Army. He took command of the revolutionary forces in Massachusetts on July 3, 1775. He was still with his troops a year later when the Declaration of Independence was signed.

4. About two hundred copies of the Declaration of Independence were made, but only twenty-six copies remain today. One lost copy was discovered behind an old picture in a frame at a flea market in 1989. It sold to a TV producer for more than eight million dollars.

5. The celebration of the Declaration of Independence was a contested issue between the Federalists and the Republicans. After the Federalist party faded away in 1812, the Declaration and its anniversary became more widely celebrated.

6. After the attack on Pearl Harbor in 1941, original copies of the Constitution and the Declaration of Independence were packed away and taken to Fort Knox for several years.

7. There is a message on the back of the Declaration of Independence, but it simply reads, "Original Declaration of Independence dated 4th July 1776."

8. When George Washington read the Declaration of Independence aloud at City Hall in New York City, a discordant group cheered the words and tore down a statue of George III. This statue was later melted down and used to create more than 42,000 musket balls for the Continental Army.

9. Only one signer, Richard Stockton, recanted his support for the revolution. Stockton was captured and jailed by the British military and worn down until he recanted. After regaining his freedom, Stockton took a new oath of loyalty to the state of New Jersey.

10. At age seventy, Benjamin Franklin was the oldest signer of the Declaration of Independence. The youngest was Edward Rutledge, who was twenty-six years old.

11. John Adams was the first person to propose that the Declaration of Independence should be celebrated with fireworks "from this time forward forever more." The *Pennsylvania Evening Post* described the first celebration in Philadelphia on

July 4, 1777 by stating: "The evening was closed with . . . a grand exhibition of fireworks (which began and concluded with thirteen rockets) on the Commons, and the city was beautifully illuminated."

The Constitution of the United States of America

We the People of the United States, in Order to form a more perfect Union, establish Justice, insure domestic Tranquility, provide for the common defence, promote the general Welfare, and secure the Blessings of Liberty to ourselves and our Posterity, do ordain and establish this Constitution for the United States of America.

Article. I.

Section. 1.

All legislative Powers herein granted shall be vested in a Congress of the United States, which shall consist of a Senate and House of Representatives.

Section. 2.

The House of Representatives shall be composed of Members chosen every second Year by the People of the several States, and the Electors in each State shall have the Qualifications requisite for Electors of the most numerous Branch of the State Legislature.

No Person shall be a Representative who shall not have attained to the Age of twenty five Years, and been seven Years a Citizen of the United States, and who shall not, when elected, be an Inhabitant of that State in which he shall be chosen.

Representatives and direct Taxes shall be apportioned among the several States which may be included within this Union, according to their respective Numbers, which shall be determined by adding to the whole Number of free Persons, including those bound to Service for a Term of Years, and excluding Indians not taxed, three fifths of all other Persons. The actual Enumeration shall be made within three Years after the first Meeting of the Congress of the United States, and within every subsequent Term of ten Years, in such Manner as they shall by Law direct. The Number of Representatives shall not exceed one for every thirty Thousand, but each State shall have at Least one Representative; and until such enumeration shall be made, the State of New Hampshire shall be entitled to chuse three, Massachusetts eight, Rhode-Island and Providence Plantations one, Connecticut five, New-York six, New Jersey four, Pennsylvania eight, Delaware one, Maryland six, Virginia ten, North Carolina five, South Carolina five, and Georgia three.

When vacancies happen in the Representation from any State, the Executive Authority thereof shall issue Writs of Election to fill such Vacancies.

The House of Representatives shall chuse their Speaker and other Officers; and shall have the sole Power of Impeachment.

Section. 3.

The Senate of the United States shall be composed of two Senators from each State, chosen by the Legislature thereof, for six Years; and each Senator shall have one Vote.

Immediately after they shall be assembled in Consequence of the first Election, they shall be divided as equally as may be into three Classes. The Seats of the Senators of the first Class shall be vacated at the Expiration of the second Year, of the second Class at the Expiration of the fourth Year, and of the third Class at the Expiration of the sixth Year, so that one third may be chosen every second Year; and if Vacancies happen by Resignation, or otherwise, during the Recess of the Legislature of any State, the Executive thereof may make temporary Appointments until the next Meeting of the Legislature, which shall then fill such Vacancies.

No Person shall be a Senator who shall not have attained to the Age of thirty Years, and been nine Years a Citizen of the United States, and who shall not, when elected, be an Inhabitant of that State for which he shall be chosen.

The Vice President of the United States shall be President of the Senate, but shall have no Vote, unless they be equally divided.

The Senate shall chuse their other Officers, and also a President pro tempore, in the Absence of the Vice President, or when he shall exercise the Office of President of the United States.

The Senate shall have the sole Power to try all Impeachments. When sitting for that Purpose, they shall be on Oath or Affirmation. When the President of the United States is tried, the Chief Justice shall preside: And no Person shall be convicted without the Concurrence of two thirds of the Members present.

Judgment in Cases of Impeachment shall not extend further than to removal from Office, and disqualification to hold and enjoy any Office of honor, Trust or Profit under the United States: but the Party convicted shall nevertheless be liable and subject to Indictment, Trial, Judgment and Punishment, according to Law.

Section. 4.

The Times, Places and Manner of holding Elections for Senators and Representatives, shall be prescribed in each State by the Legislature thereof; but the Congress may at any time by Law make or alter such Regulations, except as to the Places of chusing Senators.

The Congress shall assemble at least once in every Year, and such Meeting shall be on the first Monday in December, unless they shall by Law appoint a different Day.

Section. 5.

Each House shall be the Judge of the Elections, Returns and Qualifications of its own Members, and a Majority of each shall constitute a Quorum to do Business; but a smaller Number may adjourn from day to day, and may be authorized to compel the Attendance of absent Members, in such Manner, and under such Penalties as each House may provide.

Each House may determine the Rules of its Proceedings, punish its Members for disorderly Behaviour, and, with the Concurrence of two thirds, expel a Member.

Each House shall keep a Journal of its Proceedings, and from time to time publish the same, excepting such Parts as may in their Judgment require Secrecy; and the Yeas and Nays of the Members of either House on any question shall, at the Desire of one fifth of those Present, be entered on the Journal.

Neither House, during the Session of Congress, shall, without the Consent of the other, adjourn for more than three days, nor to any other Place than that in which the two Houses shall be sitting.

Section. 6.

The Senators and Representatives shall receive a Compensation for their Services, to be ascertained by Law, and paid out of the Treasury of the United States. They shall in all Cases, except Treason, Felony and Breach of the Peace, be privileged from Arrest during their Attendance at the Session of their respective Houses, and in going to and returning from the same; and for any Speech or Debate in either House, they shall not be questioned in any other Place.

No Senator or Representative shall, during the Time for which he was elected, be appointed to any civil Office under the Authority of the United States, which shall have been created, or the Emoluments whereof shall have been encreased during such time; and no Person holding any Office under the United States, shall be a Member of either House during his Continuance in Office.

Section. 7.

All Bills for raising Revenue shall originate in the House of Representatives; but the Senate may propose or concur with Amendments as on other Bills.

Every Bill which shall have passed the House of Representatives and the Senate, shall, before it become a Law, be presented to the President of the United States;

If he approve he shall sign it, but if not he shall return it, with his Objections to that House in which it shall have originated, who shall enter the Objections at large on their Journal, and proceed to reconsider it. If after such Reconsideration two thirds of that House shall agree to pass the Bill, it shall be sent, together with the Objections, to the other House, by which it shall likewise be reconsidered, and if approved by two thirds of that House, it shall become a Law. But in all such Cases the Votes of both Houses shall be determined by yeas and Nays, and the Names of the Persons voting for and against the Bill shall be entered on the Journal of each House respectively. If any Bill shall not be returned by the President within ten Days (Sundays excepted) after it shall have been presented to him, the Same shall be a Law, in like Manner as if he had signed it, unless the Congress by their Adjournment prevent its Return, in which Case it shall not be a Law.

Every Order, Resolution, or Vote to which the Concurrence of the Senate and House of Representatives may be necessary (except on a question of Adjournment) shall be presented to the President of the United States; and before the Same shall take Effect, shall be approved by him, or being disapproved by him, shall be repassed by two thirds of the Senate and House of Representatives, according to the Rules and Limitations prescribed in the Case of a Bill.

Section. 8.

The Congress shall have Power To lay and collect Taxes, Duties, Imposts and Excises, to pay the Debts and provide for the common Defence and general Welfare of the United States; but all Duties, Imposts and Excises shall be uniform throughout the United States;

To borrow Money on the credit of the United States;

To regulate Commerce with foreign Nations, and among the several States, and with the Indian Tribes;

To establish an uniform Rule of Naturalization, and uniform Laws on the subject of Bankruptcies throughout the United States;

To coin Money, regulate the Value thereof, and of foreign Coin, and fix the Standard of Weights and Measures;

To provide for the Punishment of counterfeiting the Securities and current Coin of the United States;

To establish Post Offices and post Roads;

To promote the Progress of Science and useful Arts, by securing for limited Times to Authors and Inventors the exclusive Right to their respective Writings and Discoveries;

To constitute Tribunals inferior to the supreme Court;

To define and punish Piracies and Felonies committed on the high Seas, and Offences against the Law of Nations;

To declare War, grant Letters of Marque and Reprisal, and make Rules concerning Captures on Land and Water;

To raise and support Armies, but no Appropriation of Money to that Use shall be for a longer Term than two Years;

To provide and maintain a Navy;

To make Rules for the Government and Regulation of the land and naval Forces;

To provide for calling forth the Militia to execute the Laws of the Union, suppress Insurrections and repel Invasions;

To provide for organizing, arming, and disciplining, the Militia, and for governing such Part of them as may be employed in the Service of the United States, reserving to the States respectively, the Appointment of the Officers, and the Authority of training the Militia according to the discipline prescribed by Congress;

To exercise exclusive Legislation in all Cases whatsoever, over such District (not exceeding ten Miles square) as may, by Cession of particular States, and the Acceptance of Congress, become the Seat of the Government of the United States, and to exercise like Authority over all Places purchased by the Consent of the Legislature of the State in which the Same shall be, for the Erection of Forts, Magazines, Arsenals, dock-Yards, and other needful Buildings;—And

To make all Laws which shall be necessary and proper for carrying into Execution the foregoing Powers, and all other Powers vested by this Constitution in the Government of the United States, or in any Department or Officer thereof.

Section. 9.

The Migration or Importation of such Persons as any of the States now existing shall think proper to admit, shall not be prohibited by the Congress prior to the Year one thousand eight hundred and eight, but a Tax or duty may be imposed on such Importation, not exceeding ten dollars for each Person.

The Privilege of the Writ of Habeas Corpus shall not be suspended, unless when in Cases of Rebellion or Invasion the public Safety may require it.

No Bill of Attainder or ex post facto Law shall be passed.

No Capitation, or other direct, Tax shall be laid, unless in Proportion to the Census or enumeration herein before directed to be taken.

No Tax or Duty shall be laid on Articles exported from any State.

No Preference shall be given by any Regulation of Commerce or Revenue to the Ports of one State over those of another: nor shall Vessels bound to, or from, one State, be obliged to enter, clear, or pay Duties in another.

No Money shall be drawn from the Treasury, but in Consequence of Appropriations made by Law; and a regular Statement and Account of the Receipts and Expenditures of all public Money shall be published from time to time.

No Title of Nobility shall be granted by the United States: And no Person holding any Office of Profit or Trust under them, shall, without the Consent of the Congress, accept of any present, Emolument, Office, or Title, of any kind whatever, from any King, Prince, or foreign State.

Section. 10.

No State shall enter into any Treaty, Alliance, or Confederation; grant Letters of Marque and Reprisal; coin Money; emit Bills of Credit; make any Thing but gold and silver Coin a Tender in Payment of Debts; pass any Bill of Attainder, ex post facto Law, or Law impairing the Obligation of Contracts, or grant any Title of Nobility.

No State shall, without the Consent of the Congress, lay any Imposts or Duties on Imports or Exports, except what may be absolutely necessary for executing it's inspection Laws: and the net Produce of all Duties and Imposts, laid by any State on Imports or Exports, shall be for the Use of the Treasury of the United States; and all such Laws shall be subject to the Revision and Controul of the Congress.

No State shall, without the Consent of Congress, lay any Duty of Tonnage, keep Troops, or Ships of War in time of Peace, enter into any Agreement or Compact with another State, or with a foreign Power, or engage in War, unless actually invaded, or in such imminent Danger as will not admit of delay.

Article. II.

Section. 1.

The executive Power shall be vested in a President of the United States of America. He shall hold his Office during the Term of four Years, and, together with the Vice President, chosen for the same Term, be elected, as follows

Each State shall appoint, in such Manner as the Legislature thereof may direct, a Number of Electors, equal to the whole Number of Senators and Representatives to which the State may be entitled in the Congress: but no Senator or Representative, or Person holding an Office of Trust or Profit under the United States, shall be appointed an Elector.

The Electors shall meet in their respective States, and vote by Ballot for two Persons, of whom one at least shall not be an Inhabitant of the same State with themselves. And they shall make a List of all the Persons voted for, and of the Number of Votes for each; which List they shall sign and certify, and transmit sealed to the Seat of the Government of the United States, directed to the President of the Senate. The President of the Senate shall, in the Presence of the Senate and House of Representatives, open all the Certificates, and the Votes shall then be counted.

The Person having the greatest Number of Votes shall be the President, if such Number be a Majority of the whole Number of Electors appointed; and if there be more than one who have such Majority, and have an equal Number of Votes, then the House of Representatives shall immediately chuse by Ballot one of them for President; and if no Person have a Majority, then from the five highest on the List the said House shall in like Manner chuse the President. But in chusing the President, the Votes shall be taken by States, the Representation from each State having one Vote; A quorum for this Purpose shall consist of a Member or Members from two thirds of the States, and a Majority of all the States shall be necessary to a Choice. In every Case, after the Choice of the President, the Person having the greatest Number of Votes of the Electors shall be the Vice President. But if there should remain two or more who have equal Votes, the Senate shall chuse from them by Ballot the Vice President.

The Congress may determine the Time of chusing the Electors, and the Day on which they shall give their Votes; which Day shall be the same throughout the United States.

No Person except a natural born Citizen, or a Citizen of the United States, at the time of the Adoption of this Constitution, shall be eligible to the Office of

President; neither shall any Person be eligible to that Office who shall not have attained to the Age of thirty five Years, and been fourteen Years a Resident within the United States.

In Case of the Removal of the President from Office, or of his Death, Resignation, or Inability to discharge the Powers and Duties of the said Office, the Same shall devolve on the Vice President, and the Congress may by Law provide for the Case of Removal, Death, Resignation or Inability, both of the President and Vice President, declaring what Officer shall then act as President, and such Officer shall act accordingly, until the Disability be removed, or a President shall be elected.

The President shall, at stated Times, receive for his Services, a Compensation, which shall neither be encreased nor diminished during the Period for which he shall have been elected, and he shall not receive within that Period any other Emolument from the United States, or any of them.

Before he enter on the Execution of his Office, he shall take the following Oath or Affirmation:—"I do solemnly swear (or affirm) that I will faithfully execute the Office of President of the United States, and will to the best of my Ability, preserve, protect and defend the Constitution of the United States."

Section. 2.

The President shall be Commander in Chief of the Army and Navy of the United States, and of the Militia of the several States, when called into the actual Service of the United States; he may require the Opinion, in writing, of the principal Officer in each of the executive Departments, upon any Subject relating to the Duties of their respective Offices, and he shall have Power to grant Reprieves and Pardons for Offences against the United States, except in Cases of Impeachment.

He shall have Power, by and with the Advice and Consent of the Senate, to make Treaties, provided two thirds of the Senators present concur; and he shall nominate, and by and with the Advice and Consent of the Senate, shall appoint Ambassadors, other public Ministers and Consuls, Judges of the supreme Court, and all other Officers of the United States, whose Appointments are not herein otherwise provided for, and which shall be established by Law: but the Congress may by Law vest the Appointment of such inferior Officers, as they think proper, in the President alone, in the Courts of Law, or in the Heads of Departments.

The President shall have Power to fill up all Vacancies that may happen during the Recess of the Senate, by granting Commissions which shall expire at the End of their next Session.

Section. 3.

He shall from time to time give to the Congress Information of the State of the Union, and recommend to their Consideration such Measures as he shall judge necessary and expedient; he may, on extraordinary Occasions, convene both Houses, or either of them, and in Case of Disagreement between them, with Respect to the Time of Adjournment, he may adjourn them to such Time as he shall think proper; he shall receive Ambassadors and other public Ministers; he shall take Care that the Laws be faithfully executed, and shall Commission all the Officers of the United States.

Section. 4.

The President, Vice President and all civil Officers of the United States, shall be removed from Office on Impeachment for, and Conviction of, Treason, Bribery, or other high Crimes and Misdemeanors.

Article. III.

Section. 1.

The judicial Power of the United States, shall be vested in one supreme Court, and in such inferior

Courts as the Congress may from time to time ordain and establish. The Judges, both of the supreme and inferior Courts, shall hold their Offices during good Behaviour, and shall, at stated Times, receive for their Services, a Compensation, which shall not be diminished during their Continuance in Office.

Section. 2.

The judicial Power shall extend to all Cases, in Law and Equity, arising under this Constitution, the Laws of the United States, and Treaties made, or which shall be made, under their Authority;—to all Cases affecting Ambassadors, other public Ministers and Consuls;—to all Cases of admiralty and maritime Jurisdiction;—to Controversies to which the United States shall be a Party;—to Controversies between two or more States;— between a State and Citizens of another State,—between Citizens of different States,—between Citizens of the same State claiming Lands under Grants of different States, and between a State, or the Citizens thereof, and foreign States, Citizens or Subjects.

In all Cases affecting Ambassadors, other public Ministers and Consuls, and those in which a State shall be Party, the supreme Court shall have original Jurisdiction. In all the other Cases before mentioned, the supreme Court shall have appellate Jurisdiction, both as to Law and Fact, with such Exceptions, and under such Regulations as the Congress shall make.

The Trial of all Crimes, except in Cases of Impeachment, shall be by Jury; and such Trial shall be held in the State where the said Crimes shall have been committed; but when not committed within any State, the Trial shall be at such Place or Places as the Congress may by Law have directed.

Section. 3.

Treason against the United States, shall consist only in levying War against them, or in adhering to their Enemies, giving them Aid and Comfort. No Person shall be convicted of Treason unless on the Testimony of two Witnesses to the same overt Act, or on Confession in open Court.

The Congress shall have Power to declare the Punishment of Treason, but no Attainder of Treason shall work Corruption of Blood, or Forfeiture except during the Life of the Person attainted.

Article. IV.

Section. 1.

Full Faith and Credit shall be given in each State to the public Acts, Records, and judicial Proceedings of every other State. And the Congress may by general Laws prescribe the Manner in which such Acts, Records and Proceedings shall be proved, and the Effect thereof.

Section. 2.

The Citizens of each State shall be entitled to all Privileges and Immunities of Citizens in the several States.

A Person charged in any State with Treason, Felony, or other Crime, who shall flee from Justice, and be found in another State, shall on Demand of the executive Authority of the State from which he fled, be delivered up, to be removed to the State having Jurisdiction of the Crime.

No Person held to Service or Labour in one State, under the Laws thereof, escaping into another, shall, in Consequence of any Law or Regulation therein, be discharged from such Service or Labour, but shall be delivered up on Claim of the Party to whom such Service or Labour may be due.

Section. 3.

New States may be admitted by the Congress into this Union; but no new State shall be formed or erected within the Jurisdiction of any other State; nor any State be formed by the Junction of two or more States, or Parts of States, without the Consent of the Legislatures of the States concerned as well as of the Congress.

The Congress shall have Power to dispose of and make all needful Rules and Regulations respecting the Territory or other Property belonging to the United States; and nothing in this Constitution shall be so construed as to Prejudice any Claims of the United States, or of any particular State.

Section. 4.

The United States shall guarantee to every State in this Union a Republican Form of Government, and shall protect each of them against Invasion; and on Application of the Legislature, or of the Executive (when the Legislature cannot be convened), against domestic Violence.

Article. V.

The Congress, whenever two thirds of both Houses shall deem it necessary, shall propose Amendments to this Constitution, or, on the Application of the Legislatures of two thirds of the several States, shall call a Convention for proposing Amendments, which, in either Case, shall be valid to all Intents and Purposes, as Part of this Constitution, when ratified by the Legislatures of three fourths of the several States, or by Conventions in three fourths thereof, as the one or the other Mode of Ratification may be proposed by the Congress; Provided that no Amendment which may be made prior to the Year One thousand eight hundred and eight shall in any Manner affect the first and fourth Clauses in the Ninth Section of the first Article; and that no State, without its Consent, shall be deprived of its equal Suffrage in the Senate.

Article. VI.

All Debts contracted and Engagements entered into, before the Adoption of this Constitution, shall be as valid against the United States under this Constitution, as under the Confederation.

This Constitution, and the Laws of the United States which shall be made in Pursuance thereof; and all Treaties made, or which shall be made, under the Authority of the United States, shall be the supreme Law of the Land; and the Judges in every State shall be bound thereby, any Thing in the Constitution or Laws of any State to the Contrary notwithstanding.

The Senators and Representatives before mentioned, and the Members of the several State Legislatures, and all executive and judicial Officers, both of the United States and of the several States, shall be bound by Oath or Affirmation, to support this Constitution; but no religious Test shall ever be required as a Qualification to any Office or public Trust under the United States.

Article. VII.

The Ratification of the Conventions of nine States, shall be sufficient for the Establishment of this Constitution between the States so ratifying the Same.

The Word, "the," being interlined between the seventh and eighth Lines of the first Page, The Word "Thirty" being partly written on an Erazure in the fifteenth Line of the first Page, The Words "is tried" being interlined between the thirty second and thirty third Lines of the first Page and the Word "the" being interlined between the forty third and forty fourth Lines of the second Page.

Attest William Jackson Secretary

done in Convention by the Unanimous Consent of the States present the Seventeenth Day of September in the Year of our Lord one thousand seven hundred and Eighty seven and of the Independance of the United States of America the Twelfth In witness whereof We have hereunto subscribed our Names,

G°. Washington
Presidt and deputy from Virginia

Delaware
Geo: Read
Gunning Bedford jun
John Dickinson
Richard Bassett
Jaco: Broom

Maryland
James McHenry
Dan of St Thos. Jenifer
Danl. Carroll

Virginia
John Blair
James Madison Jr.

North Carolina
Wm. Blount
Richd. Dobbs Spaight
Hu Williamson

South Carolina
J. Rutledge
Charles Cotesworth
Pinckney
Charles Pinckney
Pierce Butler

Georgia
William Few
Abr Baldwin

New Hampshire
John Langdon
Nicholas Gilman

Massachusetts
Nathaniel Gorham
Rufus King

Connecticut
Wm. Saml. Johnson
Roger Sherman

New York
Alexander Hamilton

New Jersey
Wil: Livingston
David Brearley
Wm. Paterson
Jona: Dayton

Pennsylvania
B Franklin
Thomas Mifflin
Robt. Morris
Geo. Clymer
Thos. FitzSimons
Jared Ingersoll
James Wilson
Gouv Morris

Context

The United States ratified its first constitution, the Articles of Confederation, in 1781. At that time, the nation was barely a loose confederation of states, each operating like an independent country. The national government was just a single body, the Congress of the Confederation, and there was no executive or judicial branch. The Articles of Confederation gave Congress the power to govern foreign affairs, conduct war, and regulate currency, but in reality, these powers were very limited because Congress had no authority to enforce its requests to the states for money or troops.

Not long after America won independence from Great Britain in 1783, it became clear that the young country needed a stronger central government in order to remain stable. In 1786, Alexander Hamilton, a lawyer and politician from New York, called for a constitutional convention to bring this strengthening to life. The Confederation Congress, which endorsed the idea in February 1787, invited all thirteen states to send delegates to a meeting in Philadelphia.

On May 25, 1787, the Constitutional Convention opened in Philadelphia at the Pennsylvania State House, now known as Independence Hall. There were fifty-five delegates representing all the states except Rhode Island, which wasn't in favor of a powerful central government. George Washington was selected as president of the convention by unanimous vote.

Congress asked the delegates to amend the Articles of Confederation, but it soon became clear that for real change to occur, they would need an entirely new government. After intense debate, which continued throughout the summer of 1787, they developed a plan that established three branches of national government: executive, legislative, and judicial. A system of checks and balances was put into place so that no single branch would have too much authority. The specific powers and responsibilities of each branch were also laid out.

Among the more controversial issues was the question of state representation in the national legislature. Delegates from larger states wanted population to determine how many representatives a state could send to Congress, while small states called for equal representation. The issue was resolved by the Connecticut Compromise, which proposed a bicameral legislature with proportional representation of the states in the lower house (House of Representatives) and equal representation in the upper house (Senate).

Another controversial topic was slavery. Although some northern states had already started to outlaw the practice, they went along with the southern states' insistence that slavery was an issue for individual states to decide and should be kept out of the Constitution. The northern delegates believed that without this compromise, the South wouldn't join the Union. For the purposes of taxation and determining how many representatives a state could send to Congress, it was decided that a slave would be counted as three-fifths of a person. Additionally, it was agreed that Congress wouldn't be allowed to prohibit the slave trade before 1808, and states were required to return fugitive slaves to their owners.

By September 1787, the convention's five-member Committee of Style had drafted the final text of the Constitution of the United States. On September 17, George Washington was the first to sign the document. Of the fifty-five delegates, a total of thirty-nine signed. Some of the delegates had already left Philadelphia, and three—George Mason and Edmund Randolph of Virginia and Elbridge Gerry of Massachusetts—refused to approve the document. In order for the Constitution to become law, it then had to be ratified by nine of the thirteen states.

James Madison and Alexander Hamilton, with assistance from John Jay, wrote a series of essays to persuade people to ratify the Constitution. The eighty-five essays, known collectively as *The Federalist Papers*, detailed how the new government would work and were published in newspapers across the states starting in the fall of 1787. People who supported the Constitution became known as Federalists, while those who opposed it—because they thought it gave too much power to the national government—were called Anti-Federalists.

Beginning on December 7, 1787, five states—Delaware, Pennsylvania, New Jersey, Georgia, and Connecticut—ratified the Constitution in quick succession. However, other states, especially Massachusetts, opposed the document, as it failed to reserve undelegated powers to the states and lacked constitutional protection of basic political rights, such as freedom of speech, religion, and the press. In February 1788, a compromise, under which Massachusetts and other states would agree to ratify the document with the assurance that amendments would be immediately proposed, was reached. The Constitution was thus narrowly ratified in Massachusetts, followed by Maryland and South Carolina. On June 21, 1788, New

Hampshire became the ninth state to ratify the document, and it was agreed that government under the Constitution would begin on March 4, 1789.

George Washington was inaugurated as America's first president on April 30, 1789. In June of that same year, Virginia ratified the Constitution, and New York followed in July. On February 2, 1790, the US Supreme Court held its first session, marking the date when the government was fully operative. Rhode Island, the last holdout of the original thirteen states, finally ratified the Constitution on May 29, 1790.

In 1789, James Madison, then a member of the US House of Representatives, introduced nineteen amendments to the Constitution. On September 25, 1789, Congress adopted twelve of the amendments and sent them to the states for ratification. Ten of these amendments, now collectively as the Bill of Rights, were ratified and became part of the Constitution on December 15, 1791. The Bill of Rights guarantees individuals certain basic protections as citizens, including freedom of speech, religion, and the press; the right to bear and keep arms; the right to peaceably assemble; protection from unreasonable search and seizure; and the right to a speedy and public trial by an impartial jury. For his contributions to the drafting of the Constitution, as well as its ratification, Madison became known as the "Father of the Constitution."

In the more than two hundred years since the Constitution was created, America has changed beyond recognition from the fledgling nation of the framers. But because of their vision and flexibility, the Constitution has endured and adapted, providing the basis for a stable nation.

Schools of Thought

Originalism vs. Living Constitution

There are two major, and often conflicting, modern theories of constitutional interpretation. Originalism is an approach that seeks to enforce the original understanding of the Constitution and sets itself against the interpretive practice known as living Constitution, which gives greater priority to contemporary needs. The debate between supporters of each school of thought is widely considered one of the most important contemporary battles over how the Constitution of the United States should be interpreted.

The basic argument for originalism is that the Constitution gets its legal effectiveness from the approval of the ratifiers. When the original Constitution was ratified, and when amendments were added to it over the course of its life, a very particular meaning was enacted, and judges should not be given the authority to change that meaning. The role of judges is to state the Constitution's original intent, not what it ought to mean. Adherence to the original understanding prevents judges from imposing their own values. In this interpretation, judges should protect a right to abortion, for example, only if the ratifiers would have agreed that it should be protected.

The basic argument for the living Constitution focuses on the fact that conditions and attitudes have changed greatly since the framers' times. Living Constitutionalists argue that the Constitution must be able to adapt in order to respond to current needs and problems rather than remaining frozen in time. Those who follow this interpretation point out that, if judicial changes were not allowed, states would still be permitted to segregate schools, ban interracial marriage, and exclude women from the practice of law, to give just a few examples.

Analysis of Quotes from the Constitution of the United States

"We the People of the United States, in Order to form a more perfect Union, establish Justice, insure domestic Tranquility, provide for the common defence, promote the general Welfare, and secure the Blessings of Liberty to ourselves and our Posterity, do ordain and establish this Constitution for the United States of America."

The preamble to the Constitution does not, unlike the rest of the document, outline specific plans for government. It is not the legally binding model that the subsequent parts are. Instead, it is an explanation of the reasons for creating the supreme law of the land. It demonstrates the wish of the framers of the Constitution to make a better, more workable, and sustainable government. They not only wanted to create something that was better than the Articles of Confederation, but also an actual nation rather than a collection of states. They also state the moral desire to ensure that the new government would be just and fair and that it would protect its citizens from internal division and from foreign attack. In keeping with the founding philosophies, the nation under the Constitution must benefit the people, rather than work against them. And, significantly, the words express a desire to accomplish these tasks for future generations of Americans.

"All legislative Powers herein granted shall be vested in a Congress of the United States, which shall consist of a Senate and House of Representatives."

Article 1 establishes the first of the three branches of the government, the Legislative branch, as a bicameral body. It defines the House of Representatives, known as the lower house of Congress. The members of the House are divided among the states proportionally, or according to size, giving more populous states more representatives. It also defines the upper house of Congress: the Senate. In the Senate, each state has equal suffrage, meaning that every state has the exact same number of senators, two each, regardless of the population. It further defines laws of election and service and details how bills become laws.

"The executive Power shall be vested in a President of the United States of America. He shall hold his Office during the Term of four Years, and, together with the Vice President, chosen for the same Term, be elected, as follows

Each State shall appoint, in such Manner as the Legislature thereof may direct, a Number of Electors, equal to the whole Number of Senators and Representatives to which the State may be entitled in the Congress: but no Senator or Representative, or Person holding an Office of Trust or Profit under the United States, shall be appointed an Elector."

Article 2 establishes the second of the three branches of government, the Executive branch. It establishes the offices of the president and the vice president, sets their terms, and determines that presidents are elected by the Electoral College, whereby each state has one vote for each member of Congress. It also sets out the powers (such as acting as commander in chief of the military, making treaties, and selecting judges), duties, and methods of removal of presidents.

"The judicial Power of the United States, shall be vested in one supreme Court, and in such inferior Courts as the Congress may from time to time ordain and establish. The Judges, both of the supreme and inferior Courts, shall hold their Offices during good Behaviour, and shall, at stated Times, receive for their Services, a Compensation, which shall not be diminished during their Continuance in Office."

Article 3 establishes the last of the three branches of government, the Judicial branch. It establishes the Supreme Court, the highest court in the United States; sets the terms of judges of both the Supreme and lower courts (good behavior has usually equated with a life term); establishes that the judges must be paid; sets the kinds of cases that may be heard by the federal judiciary and which cases the Supreme Court may hear first (called original jurisdiction); and notes that all other cases heard by the Supreme Court are by appeal. It also guarantees trial by jury in criminal court and defines the crime of treason.

"The Congress, whenever two thirds of both Houses shall deem it necessary, shall propose Amendments to this Constitution, or, on the Application of the Legisla-

tures of two thirds of the several States, shall call a Convention for proposing Amendments, which, in either Case, shall be valid to all Intents and Purposes, as Part of this Constitution, when ratified by the Legislatures of three fourths of the several States, or by Conventions in three fourths thereof, as the one or the other Mode of Ratification may be proposed by the Congress."

Article 5 details the method of amending, or changing, the Constitution. There are essentially two ways in the Constitution to propose an amendment. In the first method, a bill must pass by a two-thirds majority in each house of the legislature. Once the bill has passed both houses, it goes on to the states. This is the route that was taken by all current amendments. Because of some long-outstanding amendments, such as the twenty-seventh, Congress will normally impose a time limit (usually seven years) for a bill to be approved as an amendment.

The second method prescribed requires a constitutional convention to be called by two-thirds of the legislatures of the states and for that convention to propose one or more amendments. These amendments are then sent to the states to be approved by three-fourths of the legislatures or conventions. This option has never been exercised, and there is speculation about just how such a convention would be convened and what kind of changes it would create.

Regardless of which of the two proposal routes is taken, an amendment must be ratified, or approved, by three-fourths of the states. The text of the amendment may specify whether the bill must be passed by the state legislatures or by a state convention, but are sent to the legislatures of the states by default. Only one amendment, the twenty-first, specified a convention. In any case, passage by the legislature or convention is by simple majority.

Analysis of Quotes About the Constitution of the United States

"*The strength of the Constitution lies entirely in the determination of each citizen to defetnd it. Only if every single citizen feels duty bound to do his share in this defense are the constitutional rights secure.*"

—Albert Einstein

Einstein, writing during the era of Joseph McCarthy's influence, expresses his belief that the American people must be involved in their government. The Constitution itself has no power if there is no one to stand up for it. What gives the Constitution its authority is the dedication of citizens to upholding the rights enshrined therein. Einstein warns that our constitutional rights are endangered by an apathetic population.

"We . . . the people . . . are the rightful masters of both Congresses, and courts—not to overthrow the Constitution, but to overthrow the men who pervert it."

—Abraham Lincoln,
September 16, 1859

In a campaign speech, Lincoln discussed slavery in terms of the Constitution and the rights it granted to states. His argument here is that, while the Constitution can be used to protect rights and behaviors that are immoral (such as slavery), it is the responsibility of the people to make sure it is not used in such a manner. Citizens of the United States must understand what the Constitution allows and recognize the limits of its rulings. Only by knowing what it says can we fight back against those who would use the Constitution as a means to an immoral end.

"The Constitution is colorblind, and neither knows nor tolerates classes among citizens."
—Supreme Court Justice John Marshall Harlan

Harlan was the lone dissenter in Plessy v. Ferguson in 1896, which found that "separate but equal" rules for black and white citizens were constitutional. (This finding was later overturned by Brown v. Board of Education.) Harlan's famous dissent, from which this quote is taken, implies that racial, gender, and class discrimination is something invented by people, not the Constitution. The rights outlined by the Founding Fathers are meant to apply equally to every citizen.

"It is therefore peculiarly true of constitutional govern-ment that its atmosphere is opinion. . . . It does not remain fixed in any unchanging form, but grows with the growth and is altered with the change of the nation's needs and purposes." —Woodrow Wilson,
March 24, 1908

Wilson, a political science scholar and America's twenty-eighth president, contends that the Constitution of the United States is the building block of our government, but it was never meant to be forever unchanged. It is designed to be amended as the times demand, such as with the abolition of slavery, the granting of civil rights, or giving women the right to vote.

"Our constitution works. Our great republic is a government of laws, not of men." —Gerald R. Ford, August 9, 1974

President Ford made this statement in reference to the resignation of his predecessor, Richard Nixon. Nixon, facing impeachment over the Watergate scandal, had left office under a cloud of suspicion, accused of trying to use his power to escape prosecution. Ford's quote illuminates the concept that no person, not even the president, is outside the scope of the Constitution. The laws apply equally to every citizen.

Trivia

1. Since the ratification of the Constitution, and the inclusion of the Bill of Rights, more than 11,000 amendments have been proposed.

2. It is extremely difficult to pass a constitutional amendment. The last amendment ratified was the Twenty-Seventh Amendment, which states, "No law, varying the compensation for the services of the Senators and Representatives, shall take effect, until an election of Representatives shall have intervened." It was proposed on September 25, 1789; it became a law on May 7, 1992, nearly 203 years later.

3. At just 4,400 words, the Constitution of the United States is the oldest and shortest constitution of any major government in the world.

4. Pennsylvania's own delegate misspelled the state's name when he signed the Constitution. It is also misspelled on the Liberty Bell.

5. The only presidents to sign the Constitution were George Washington and James Madison.

6. The word *democracy* is not found in the Constitution, as the men at the Constitutional Convention felt pure democracy was a dangerous form of government.

7. John Shallus, a clerk for the Pennsylvania General Assembly, was tasked with writing out the Constitution. He was paid thirty dollars to transcribe the four pages of the document on vellum parchment using a quill pen.

8. Constitution Day is celebrated on September 17, the anniversary of the day the framers signed the document.

9. At the time of the signing, the population of the United States was four million. Based on recent estimates, it is now more than 326 million.

The Bill of Rights

PREAMBLE TO THE BILL OF RIGHTS

Congress of the United States
begun and held at the City of New-York, on Wednesday the fourth of March, one thousand seven hundred and eighty nine.

THE Conventions of a number of the States, having at the time of their adopting the Constitution, expressed a desire, in order to prevent misconstruction or abuse of its powers, that further declaratory and restrictive clauses should be added: And as extending the ground of public confidence in the Government, will best ensure the beneficent ends of its institution.

RESOLVED by the Senate and House of Representatives of the United States of America, in Congress assembled, two thirds of both Houses concurring, that the following Articles be proposed to the Legislatures of the several States, as amendments to the Constitution of the United States, all, or any of which Articles, when ratified by three fourths of the said Legislatures, to be valid to all intents and purposes, as part of the said Constitution; viz.

ARTICLES in addition to, and Amendment of the Constitution of the United States of America, proposed by Congress, and ratified by the Legislatures of the several States, pursuant to the fifth Article of the original Constitution.

AMENDMENTS RATIFIED ON DECEMBER 15, 1791: THE BILL OF RIGHTS

Amendment I

Congress shall make no law respecting an establishment of religion, or prohibiting the free exercise thereof; or abridging the freedom of speech, or of the press; or the right of the people peaceably to assemble, and to petition the Government for a redress of grievances.

Amendment II

A well regulated Militia, being necessary to the security of a free State, the right of the people to keep and bear Arms, shall not be infringed.

Amendment III

No Soldier shall, in time of peace be quartered in any house, without the consent of the Owner, nor in time of war, but in a manner to be prescribed by law.

Amendment IV

The right of the people to be secure in their persons, houses, papers, and effects, against unreasonable searches and seizures, shall not be violated, and no Warrants shall issue, but upon probable cause, supported by Oath or affirmation, and particularly describing the place to be searched, and the persons or things to be seized.

Amendment V

No person shall be held to answer for a capital, or otherwise infamous crime, unless on a presentment or indictment of a Grand Jury, except in cases arising in the land or naval forces, or in the Militia, when in actual service in time of War or public danger; nor shall any person be subject for the same offence to be twice put in jeopardy of life or limb; nor shall be compelled in any criminal case to be a witness against himself, nor be deprived of life, liberty, or property, without due process of law; nor shall private property be taken for public use, without just compensation.

Amendment VI

In all criminal prosecutions, the accused shall enjoy the right to a speedy and public trial, by an impartial jury of the State and district wherein the crime shall have been committed, which district shall have been previously ascertained by law, and to be informed of the nature and cause of the accusation; to be confronted with the witnesses against him; to have compulsory process for obtaining witnesses in his favor, and to have the Assistance of Counsel for his defence.

Amendment VII

In Suits at common law, where the value in controversy shall exceed twenty dollars, the right of trial by jury shall be preserved, and no fact tried by a jury, shall be otherwise re-examined in any Court of the United States, than according to the rules of the common law.

Amendment VIII

Excessive bail shall not be required, nor excessive fines imposed, nor cruel and unusual punishments inflicted.

Amendment IX

The enumeration in the Constitution, of certain rights, shall not be construed to deny or disparage others retained by the people.

Amendment X

The powers not delegated to the United States by the Constitution, nor prohibited by it to the States, are reserved to the States respectively, or to the people.

Context

The Bill of Rights is the first ten amendments to the Constitution of the United States, but both the name and the basic ideas are founded in English history. In 1215, a group of barons made King John agree to the Magna Carta, or Great Charter, a written document protecting subjects against royal abuses of power and upholding a "law of the land." In 1628, Parliament adopted the Petition of Right, condemning unlawful imprisonments and providing that there would be no tax "without common consent of Parliament." In 1689, Parliament adopted the Bill of Rights. The name of the American document derives from this, as do some of its ideas. For example, just as in our Eighth Amendment, the Parliamentary Bill calls for a ban on excessive bails and fines and forbids cruel and unusual punishment.

The American colonists adopted the idea of written documents protecting individual liberties early on. Colonial charters, such as the 1606 Charter for Virginia, declared that colonists should enjoy the same "privileges, franchises, and immunities" as they would in England. Americans continued to write tracts and resolutions, especially after the Stamp Act of 1765, basing their claim of rights on the Magna Carta, the Parliamentary Bill, the colonial charters, and the teachings of natural law.

After declaring their independence in 1776, the American states turned to writing state constitutions and state bills of rights. George Mason was the principal shaper of Virginia's Declaration of Rights. That declaration, which took John Locke's opinions on natural rights and combined them with real protections against specific abuses, was the model for bills of rights in other states and, ultimately, for the federal Bill of Rights. Mason's declaration was also influential in the framing of France's Declaration of the Rights of Man and of the Citizen in 1789.

In 1787, at the Constitutional Convention in Philadelphia, Mason expressed a wish that the document had been prefaced by a Bill of Rights. Elbridge Gerry moved for the appointment of a committee to prepare such a bill, but the delegates, without debate, defeated the motion. They did not oppose the principle of a bill of rights, but they thought it was unnecessary because the new federal government would have only specifically stated powers. Some of the framers of the Constitution also questioned the usefulness of what James Madison called "parchment barriers" against majorities, and they looked for protection to practical structural fixtures such as separation of powers and checks and balances.

Opponents of ratification soon focused on the absence of a bill of rights, and Federalists, especially Madison, quickly realized they had to offer to add amendments to the Constitution after its ratification. Only by making this pledge were the Constitution's supporters able to achieve ratification in such divided states as New York and Virginia.

At the first session of the US Congress, Madison set about carrying out his promise. He painstakingly crafted amendments from among the numerous proposals made in the state-ratifying conventions. Madison faced many obstacles, such as the lack of interest from some members who thought the House had more important work to do, and outright hostility on the part of Anti-Federalists who hoped for a second convention to hobble the powers of the federal government. But in September 1789, the House and Senate accepted a conference report laying out the language of proposed amendments to the Constitution.

Within six months, these amendments, which were to become the Bill of Rights, had been submitted to the states, and nine had ratified them. By December 15, 1791, with Virginia's ratification, the Bill of Rights became part of the Constitution. Ten amendments were ratified; two others, dealing with the number of representatives and with the compensation of senators and representatives, were not.

The Bill of Rights established soaring principles that guaranteed the most fundamental rights in very general terms. The basic rights that the document was created to protect, and which were believed to be "natural rights," included:

- **Freedom of Religion:** the right to exercise one's own religion, or no religion, free from any government influence or compulsion;
- **Freedom of Speech, Press, Petition, and Assembly:** under which even unpopular expression is protected from government suppression or censorship;
- **Privacy:** the right to be free of unwarranted and unwanted government intrusion into one's personal and private affairs, papers, and possessions;
- **Due Process of Law:** the right to be treated fairly by the government whenever the loss of liberty or property is at stake; and

- **Equality Before the Law:** the right to be treated equally before the law, regardless of social status.

The original Constitution has been amended a number of times—for example, to provide for direct election of senators and to give eighteen-year-olds the right to vote. The Bill of Rights, however, has never been amended. There is, of course, a great deal of debate over Supreme Court interpretation of specific provisions, especially where social interests (i.e., the control of drug trafficking) seem to come into tension with provisions of the Bill of Rights, such as the Fourth Amendment. Despite these debates, and sometimes as a result of them, the Bill of Rights lies at the heart of American conceptions of individual liberty and protections; limits to the authority of government; and the rule of law.

Analysis of Quotes from the Bill of Rights

"Congress shall make no law respecting an establishment of religion, or prohibiting the free exercise thereof; or abridging the freedom of speech, or of the press; or the right of the people peaceably to assemble, and to petition the Government for a redress of grievances."

The First Amendment guarantees the separation of Church and State. The government cannot dictate how citizens worship or prevent someone from worshipping. This was intended to prevent the imposition of a state religion, or religious "tests" for office, as happened frequently in Europe. The amendment also protects the citizens' right to speak their conscience without fear of reprisal and gives the press the same protection. Furthermore, it protects the right of citizens to petition, or complain to the government, without fear of arrest or persecution. The free interchange promoted by this amendment is fundamental to the American perception of freedom.

"A well regulated Militia, being necessary to the security of a free State, the right of the people to keep and bear Arms, shall not be infringed."

The controversial Second Amendment states that, in light of the need for a militia, citizens have a right to own guns. In the eighteenth century, a militia was indeed necessary to defend against attacks from Native Americans and hostile foreign powers. Once the United States possessed the most powerful standing army in the world, not to mention a well-regulated militia that provided guns for its members (the National Guard), the need for this arguably diminished. Another reason for the creation of this amendment was the regulation of gun ownership by European monarchs. Americans being free people, gun ownership was seen as an emblem of that liberty.

As technology and society change, this amendment will no doubt continue to be debated.

"The right of the people to be secure in their persons, houses, papers, and effects, against unreasonable searches and seizures, shall not be violated, and no Warrants shall issue, but upon probable cause, supported by Oath or affirmation, and particularly describing the place to be searched, and the persons or things to be seized."

The Fourth Amendment states that no one can enter an individual's house without either permission or a search warrant. In order to obtain a search warrant, one must have legal justification. The warrant must be authorized and documented and it must state specifically the place being searched and what is being looked for. This amendment shows not only the importance of property rights to the Founding Fathers, but also their desire to make the protection of the individual concrete.

"In all criminal prosecutions, the accused shall enjoy the right to a speedy and public trial, by an impartial jury of the State and district wherein the crime shall have been committed, which district shall have been previously ascertained by law, and to be informed of the nature and cause of the accusation; to be confronted

with the witnesses against him; to have compulsory process for obtaining witnesses in his favor, and to have the Assistance of Counsel for his defence."

The basic purpose of the Sixth Amendment is to prevent the government from detaining citizens unfairly. This was in reaction to European secret courts and detentions. The amendment further states that citizens have a right to a speedy and public trial and to be tried fairly and near the same location they were arrested. The accused must also be told what it is they're being tried for, know who is testifying against them, and have the right to provide witnesses and to have an attorney for their own defense. This all reinforces the concept that the individual has sacrosanct rights, and it is the job of the law to protect them.

"The enumeration in the Constitution, of certain rights, shall not be construed to deny or disparage others retained by the people."

Many framers of the Constitution of the United States did not feel a Bill of Rights was necessary. They argued that these justices are not granted by the government, as they are natural rights. Others feared that rights not specifically listed could be taken away. The Ninth Amendment calmed their fears by emphasizing that rights not necessarily listed by the Constitution cannot be taken away by the government. This has also been valuable as it allows lawmakers to expand the protections offered under the law.

Analysis of Quotes About the Bill of Rights

"Without their determined opposition, however, the first ten amendments would not have become a part of the Constitution for later generations to transform into a powerful instrument for the defense of American freedom. . . . Their example might well be their greatest gift to posterity."   —Pauline Maier, *Ratification: The People Debate the Constitution, 1787–1788*

Author Pauline Maier refers to the critics of the Constitution who successfully pushed for a bill of rights to be added. Without the Bill of Rights, our media would not have the freedom to print news as it is happening instead of a releasing filtered versions approved by those in power. Similar statements can be made about the freedom to practice (or not practice) religion, the expected right of privacy within your home, and all the other protections contained within the Bill of Rights. These amendments safeguard our most cherished freedoms.

"A bill of rights is what the people are entitled to against every government on earth, general or particular, and what no just government should refuse."
—Thomas Jefferson,
December 20, 1787

In a letter to James Madison, who would later become the author of the Bill of Rights, Jefferson notes that he is unhappy that the Constitution (which had been signed but not yet ratified) did not include a bill of rights. As one of the Founding Fathers, Jefferson knew what it was like to live in a country where freedoms were threatened, and he felt there should be a clear delineation of basic rights such as freedom of the press and of religion and the right to trial by jury. He ultimately got what he wanted: The Bill of Rights clearly outlines our protections against the government as citizens of the United States.

"If this nation is to be wise as well as strong, if we are to achieve our destiny, then we need more new ideas for more wise men reading more good books in more public libraries. These libraries should be open to all—except the censor. We must know all the facts and hear all the alternatives and listen to all the criticisms. Let us welcome controversial books and controversial authors. For the Bill of Rights is the guardian of our security as well as our liberty." —John F. Kennedy, October 29, 1960

Writing shortly before his election as president, Kennedy speaks of libraries and of censorship in the form of book banning. Though books can, in very specific circumstances, be blocked from schools, for the most part, the First Amendment protects them from removal. Kennedy's point is that the protections of the Bill of Rights allows for the education of citizens: We must be able to learn from what is around us and what materials we have available, and we cannot do so under censorship.

"We will not, under any threat, or in the face of any danger, surrender the guarantees of liberty our forefathers framed for us in our Bill of Rights." —Franklin D. Roosevelt, December 15, 1941

President Roosevelt spoke in a radio address a week after the attack on Pearl Harbor, commemorating the 150th anniversary of the ratification of the Bill of Rights. His fiery speech indicted the fascist rulers of Germany, Japan, and Italy and referred repeatedly to Hitler's rejection of the freedoms set forth in the Bill of Rights. His quote remains as true today as it was then: The moment that we, as Americans, relinquish our hold on the liberties provided to us in the Bill of Rights, we lose our democracy. Despite the fear gripping the nation at the time of his speech, Roosevelt maintained that Americans had to stand strong and remain confident that their liberties would be upheld.

"Who needs the protection of the Bill of Rights most? The weak, the most vulnerable in society." —Danny Kaye

In 1981, actor Danny Kaye starred in the TV movie *Skokie*, about the fight over whether or not a neo-Nazi group had the right to demonstrate in a Jewish community in Illinois. His quote about the importance of the Bill of Rights responds to the First Amendment issues raised in that case. The Bill of Rights was not written to safeguard the powerful members of society, but rather the weakest members, who cannot protect themselves. The most vulnerable members in the social order must rely on the protections afforded to them by the Bill of Rights.

Trivia

1. On November 27, 1941, President Franklin D. Roosevelt declared December 15 to be Bill of Rights Day; however, the first celebration of the holiday was observed solemnly due to the attack on Pearl Harbor. It remains a federal holiday, despite its relative obscurity.

2. North Carolina's original copy of the Bill of Rights went missing during the Civil War but was recovered by an undercover FBI agent in 2003.

3. The Bill of Rights was proposed because the Constitution outlined what the US government could

do, but not what it could *not* do. It was necessary to provide specifications on the limits of government power.

4. George Washington commissioned fourteen copies of the Bill of Rights, one for the federal government and one for each of the thirteen original states—eight of which are still safely secured in their respective states. The copies belonging to Georgia and New York were probably burned; Pennsylvania's copy was likely stolen in the late nineteenth century; Delaware signed the copy sent to them and mailed it back, and it is now part of the National Archives; and Maryland doesn't know what happened to its copy. Two have resurfaced, one of which may be Pennsylvania's missing copy.

5. George Mason, whose "Declaration of Rights" for Virginia greatly influenced James Madison's writing, refused to sign the Constitution because it created a government he felt might be too powerful, it did not abolish slavery, and there was no bill of rights. Mason was the most vocal advocate for a bill of rights.

6. The National Constitution Center displays one of the twelve surviving original copies of the Bill of Rights.

7. Part of the argument surrounding the Bill of Rights, and the ratification of the Constitution, was about who would enforce the Constitution and make the final decisions on what is and is not constitutional.

8. James Madison originally proposed nineteen amendments. The House advanced seventeen of them, and the Senate passed only twelve to the states for ratification.

9. Of the two proposed amendments that were not ratified in 1791, the original second amendment (regarding salary for members of Congress) was ratified as the Constitution's Twenty-Seventh Amendment in 1992.

10. Connecticut, Massachusetts, and Georgia did not ratify the Bill of Rights until 1939.

About the Founding Fathers

John Adams: In 1774, John Adams served in the Second Continental Congress and was part of the five-man team that drafted the Declaration of Independence. In 1779, he was one of the American diplomats sent to negotiate the Treaty of Paris. Adams remained in Europe after the war, negotiating treaties of commerce with many European nations. He was appointed the first US minister to England in 1785. Like Thomas Jefferson, Adams was abroad during the creation of the Constitution of the United States, but he made sure to provide his input to the delegates at the Constitutional Convention. After serving two terms as Washington's vice president, John Adams won the presidency in 1796.

Benjamin Franklin: In 1775, Benjamin Franklin was elected to the Second Continental Congress, became the first postmaster general for the colonies, and was appointed to the five-man team that contributed to the writing of the Declaration of Independence. He was later elected commissioner to France and was a key negotiator for the 1783 Treaty of Paris, which ended the Revolutionary War. In 1787, after his return to the United States, Franklin was elected to represent Pennsylvania at the Constitutional Convention. He was the oldest delegate at the convention and is credited with helping to fashion the Connecticut Compromise, which balanced representation in Congress between large and small states through the creation of the House of Representatives.

Alexander Hamilton: In 1787, Alexander Hamilton was invited to participate in the Constitutional Convention as the New York delegate. While he did not have a strong hand in writing the Constitution, he had a large role in ratifying it. Joined by James Madison and John Jay, Hamilton wrote fifty-one of the eighty-five essays titled *The Federalist Papers*. After the ratification of the Constitution, he was appointed as the first secretary of the treasury under George Washington.

John Hancock: After British customs officials seized one of his merchant ships, the *Liberty*, Hancock became increasingly involved in the movement for American independence. In 1765, Hancock was elected Boston selectman. He later went on to hold a position in the Massachusetts colonial legislature, which led to his appointment as president of the Second Continental Congress in 1775. Hancock is credited as the first signer of the Declaration of Independence and his bold signature was supposedly inscribed so that the English king would not need glasses to read it. In 1780, he was elected the first governor of the Commonwealth of Massachusetts and helped frame the Massachusetts Constitution adopted that same year. Hancock lost the first US presidential election to George Washington in 1789, but he remained the governor of Massachussets until his death in 1793.

Thomas Jefferson: When Thomas Jefferson attended the Second Continental Congress, he was appointed to the five-man team that contributed to the writing of the Declaration of Independence. After the Declaration of Independence, Jefferson served as a member of the Virginia House of Delegates from 1776 to 1779, the second governor of Virginia from 1779 to

1781, and the US minister to France from 1785 to 1789. Despite being in France when the Constitution was being drafted, Jefferson kept in close contact with James Madison to ensure his opinions and influence on the supreme law of the land.

Robert Livingston: Although not regarded as a founding father, Robert Livingston served as a New York State representative during the Continental Congress. He became one of five men appointed to write the Declaration of Independence but was called away from the congress before the document was signed. Livingston later helped create New York's state constitution and became the state's chancellor. In 1788, Livingston worked with Alexander Hamilton to ensure his home state of New York ratified the new constitution. Later, Livingston served as the US minister to France and worked with James Monroe on the details of the Louisiana Purchase.

James Madison: After receiving an appointment to draft Virginia's constitution, James Madison represented Virginia at the Constitutional Convention in 1787. In the Virginia Plan, Madison expressed his ideas about a three-part central government, consisting of executive, legislative, and judicial branches. He also suggested a system of checks and balances to prevent one branch from having too much power over the others. When the Constitution faced opposition from Virginia and other colonies, Madison joined John Jay and Alexander Hamilton in writing *The Federalist Papers*, supporting the proposed set of laws. After winning a seat in the House of Representatives in 1789, Madison submitted his suggested amendments to the 1789 Constitutional Convention. He proposed seventeen amendments, twelve of which made it through to the states and ten which were ratified and became the Bill of Rights. Madison served as Thomas Jefferon's secretary of state in 1801 and became the fourth president of the United States in 1809.

George Mason: While George Mason was not involved in writing the Bill of Rights, his 1776 Virginia Declaration of Rights heavily influenced James Madison's proposed amendments.

Benjamin Rush: On July 20, 1776, Benjamin Rush was appointed Pennsylvania's representative in Congress. He signed the Declaration of Independence on August 2, 1776, the only signer with a medical degree. In 1777, he was appointed Surgeon General of the Middle Continental Army. His last involvement in politics was in 1789, when he and James Wilson successfully reformed the Pennsylvania constitution. Rush also helped organize the first anti-slavery society in America: the Pennsylvania Society for Promoting the Abolition of Slavery and the Relief of Free Negroes Unlawfully Held in Bondage.

Roger Sherman: From 1774–1781 and 1783–1784, Roger Sherman served in the First and Second Continental Congresses. Although not regarded a founding father, during his service, Sherman was appointed to the five-man team that contributed to the creation of the Declaration of Independence and helped write the Articles of Confederation. At the Constitutional Convention, Sherman introduced the Connecticut Compromise, also known as the Great Compromise, to address the issue of states' representation in the federal government. He was a supporter of Alexander Hamilton's call for a national bank and protective tariffs and earned the respect of Thomas Jefferson and John Adams. Sherman later served in the House of Representatives and then became a US senator.

Bibliography

"Abraham Lincoln Papers at the Library of Congress." Library of Congress. Accessed April 13, 2017. https://www.loc.gov/teachers /classroommaterials/connections/abraham-lincoln-papers/history3.html.

Armitage, David. *The Declaration of Independence: A Global History*. Cambridge, MA: Harvard University Press, 2007.

Bailyn, Bernard, ed. *The Debate on the Constitution: Federalist and Antifederalist Speeches, Articles, and Letters During the Struggle for Ratification. Part Two: January to August 1788*. The Library of America, 1993.

Bailyn, Bernard. *The Ideological Origins of the American Revolution.* Enlarged edition. Cambridge, MA: Harvard University Press, 1992.

Becker, Carl. *The Declaration of Independence: A Study in the History of Political Ideas.* Revised edition. New York: Vintage Books, 1970.

"Bill of Rights of the United States of America (1791)." Bill of Rights Institute. Accessed April 04, 2017. https://www.billofrightsinstitute.org/founding-documents/bill-of-rights/.

Billias, George Athan. *American Constitutionalism Heard Round the World, 1776-1989: A Global Perspective.* New York: New York University Press, 2009.

Biography.com Editors. "Alexander Hamilton Biography.com." Accessed April 4, 2017. http://www.biography.com/people/alexander-hamilton-9326481.

———. "Benjamin Franklin Biography.com." Accessed April 4, 2017. http://www.biography.com/people/benjamin-franklin-9301234

———. "James Madison Biography.com." Accessed April 4, 2017. http://www.biography.com/people/james-madison-9394965.

———. "Benjamin Rush Biography.com." Accessed June 8, 2017. http://www.biography.com/people/benjaminrush-9467074

———. "John Adams Biography.com." Accessed April 04, 2017. http://www.biography.com /people/john-adams-37967.

———. "Robert R. Livingston Biography.com." Accessed April 04, 2017. http://www.biography .com/people/robert-r-livingston-9383941.

———. "Roger Sherman Biography.com." Accessed April 4, 2017. http://www.biography.com/people /roger-sherman-9482029.

———. "Thomas Jefferson. Biography.com." Accessed April 04, 2017. http://www.biography.com /people/thomas-jefferson-9353715.

Bowen, Catherine. *Miracle at Philadelphia: The Story of the Constitutional Convention, May to September 1787.* New York: Little, Brown, 2010.

Boyd, Julian P. (ed.) *The Declaration of Independence: The Evolution of the Text.* Revised edition edited by Gerard W. Gawalt. Washington, DC: Library of Congress, 1999.

———. *The Papers of Thomas Jefferson,* Vol. 1. Princeton: Princeton University Press, 1950.

Bradshaw, William B. "Trivia: Seven Questions and Answers about the Declaration of Independence." *The Huffington Post.* Accessed June 8, 2017. http://www.huffingtonpost.com /william-b-bradshaw/trivia-seven-declaration-of-independence_b_5580161.html.

Bryce, Viscount James, *The American Commonwealth.*

Vol. 1, 2nd ed., London: Macmillan and Co., 1888.

Burnett, Edward Cody. *The Continental Congress.* New York: Norton, 1941 "Declaration of Independence: A Transcription." National Archives and Records Administration. Accessed March 28, 2017. https://www.archives.gov /founding-docs/declaration-transcript.

Carter, Joe. "5 Facts About the Bill of Rights." December 15, 2016. Acton Institute PowerBlog. Accessed April 11, 2017. http://blog.acton.org /archives/90718-5-facts-about-the-bill-of-rights-2.html.

Casey, Gregory. "The Supreme Court and Myth: An Empirical Investigation." *Law & Society Review.* 8(3): 385–420. doi:10.2307/3053081. JSTOR 3053081.

Christie, Ian R., and Benjamin W. Labaree. *Empire or Independence, 1760–1776: A British-American Dialogue on the Coming of the American Revolution.* New York: Norton, 1976.

Deseret News. "25 Historical Quotes about the Declaration of Independence, July 4th and America." DeseretNews.com. Accessed April 13, 2017. http://www.deseretnews.com/top/2597/6 /July-1776-25-historical-quotes-about-the-Declaration-of-Independence-July-4th-and-America.html.

Detweiler, Philip F. "The Changing Reputation of the Declaration of Independence: The First Fifty Years." *William and Mary Quarterly*, 3rd series, 19(1962): 557–74.

Dumbauld, Edward. *The Declaration of Independence And What It Means Today*. Norman, OK: University of Oklahoma Press, 1950.

Dupont, Christian Y., and Peter S. Onuf, eds. *Declaring Independence: The Origins and Influence of America's Founding Document*. Revised edition. Charlottesville, VA: University of Virginia Library, 2010.

Ellis, Joseph. *American Creation: Triumphs and Tragedies at the Founding of the Republic*. New York: Knopf, 2007.

Farber, Daniel. *Lincoln's Constitution*. Chicago: University of Chicago Press, 2003.

"Fascinating Facts about the Declaration of Independence." Accessed April 04, 2017. https://www.constitutionfacts.com/us-declaration-of-independence/fascinating-facts/.

"Fascinating Facts about the U.S. Constitution." Accessed April 13, 2017. https://www.constitutionfacts.com/us-constitution-amendments/fascinating-facts/.

Ferling, John E. *A Leap in the Dark: The Struggle to Create the American Republic*. New York: Oxford University Press, 2003.

Ford, Paul Leicester, ed. *Pamphlets on the Constitution of the United States: Published During its Discussion by the People, 1787–1788*. Clark, NJ: Lawbook Exchange Ltd., 2010.

Fritz, Christian G. *American Sovereigns: The People and America's Constitutional Tradition Before the Civil War*. New York: Cambridge University Press, 2008.

GRFordLibraryMuseum. "Swearing in Ceremony of Gerald R. Ford as 38th President of the United States, August 9. 1974." YouTube. July 16, 2012. Accessed April 13, 2017. https://www.youtube.com/watch?v=H5qExW0HFCI.

Gustafson, Milton. "Travels of the Charters of Freedom." *Prologue*. Winter 2002, Vol. 34, no. 4.

Hall, Kermit. *The Oxford Companion to the Supreme Court of the United States*. New York: Oxford University Press, 1992.

Harrison, Elizabeth. "9 Things You May Not Know About the Declaration of Independence." History.com. July 4, 2012. Accessed April 13, 2017. http://www.history.com/news/9-things-you-may-not-know-about-the-declaration-of-independence.

Hazelton, John H. *The Declaration of Independence: Its History*. New York: Da Capo Press, 1970.

History.com Staff. "8 Things You Should Know About the Bill of Rights." History.com. December 10, 2015. Accessed April 04, 2017. http://www

.history.com/news/history-lists/8-things-you-should-know-about-the-bill-of-rights.

———. "John Hancock." 2009. Accessed June 8, 2017. http://www.history.com/topics/american-revolution/john-hancock

———. "The U.S. Constitution." History.com. 2009. Accessed April 4, 2017. http://www.history.com/topics/constitution.

———. "Writing of Declaration of Independence." History.com. 2010. Accessed April 4, 2017. http://www.history.com/topics/american-revolution/writing-of-declaration-of-independence.

Jensen, Merrill. *The Founding of a Nation: A History of the American Revolution, 1763–1776*. New York: Oxford University Press, 1968.

"John Adams to Abigail Adams, 3 July 1776." National Archives and Records Administration. Accessed April 13, 2017. https://founders.archives.gov/documents/Adams/04-02-02-0016.

"John F. Kennedy Speeches." John F. Kennedy Presidential Library and Museum. Accessed April 13, 2017. https://www.jfklibrary.org/Research/Research-Aids/JFK-Speeches/Milwaukee-WI_19590409.aspx.

Journals of the Continental Congress, 1774–1789, Vol. 5. Washington, DC: Library of Congress, 1904–1937.

Klein, Christopher. "7 Things You May Not Know About the Constitutional Convention." History.

com. September 17, 2012. Accessed April 4, 2017. http://www.history.com/news/7-things-you-may-not-know-about-the-constitutional-convention.

Levy, Leonard W., Kenneth L. Karst, and John G. West, eds. *Encyclopedia of the American Constitution.* New York: Macmillan, 1992.

Lucas, Stephen E., "Justifying America: The Declaration of Independence as a Rhetorical Document", in Thomas W. Benson, ed., *American Rhetoric: Context and Criticism*, Carbondale, IL: Southern Illinois University Press, 1989

Maier, Pauline. *American Scripture: Making the Declaration of Independence.* New York: Knopf, 1997.

———. *Ratification: The People Debate the Constitution, 1787–1788.* New York: Simon & Schuster, 2010.

Malone, Dumas. *Jefferson the Virginian.* Boston: Little Brown, 1948.

Marshall, John. "Plessy v. Ferguson (1896)." LII / Legal Information Institute. August 19, 2010. Accessed April 13, 2017. https://www.law.cornell.edu/wex/plessy_v._ferguson_1896.

Mayer, David. "Declaration of Independence." In Hamowy, Ronald. *The Encyclopedia of Libertarianism.* Thousand Oaks, CA: SAGE; Cato Institute., 2008. doi:10.4135/9781412965811. n72. ISBN 978-1-4129-6580-4.

McDonald, Forrest. *Novus Ordo Seclorum: The Intellectual Origins of the Constitution.* Lawrence: University Press of Kansas, 1985.

McDonald, Robert M. S. "Thomas Jefferson's Changing Reputation as Author of the Declaration of Independence: The First Fifty Years." *Journal of the Early Republic* 19, no. 2 (Summer 1999): 169–95.

McPherson, James. *Abraham Lincoln and the Second American Revolution.* New York: Oxford University Press, 1991.

Middlekauff, Robert. *The Glorious Cause: The American Revolution, 1763–1789.* Revised and expanded edition. New York: Oxford University Press, 2005.

Moncure, Thomas M., Jr. "Who is the Militia: The Virginia Ratification Convention and the Right to Bear Arms." *Lincoln Law Review* 19: 1–25. Retrieved November 11, 2011.

Munson, Holly. "FAQ: Basic Facts About the Bill of Rights." National Constitution Center. Accessed April 4, 2017. https://constitutioncenter.org/blog/everything-you-ever-wanted-to-know-about-the-bill-of-rights.

NCC Staff. "10 Fascinating Facts About the Declaration of Independence." National Constitution Center. Accessed April 13, 2017. https://constitutioncenter.org/blog/10-fascinating-facts-about-the-declaration-of-independence.

Norton, Mary Beth, et al., *A People and a Nation*, Eighth Edition, Boston, Wadsworth, 2010.

O'Connor, Tom. "A Guide to Constitutional Structure." July 6, 2006. Retrieved November 14, 2011. https://www.merlot.org/merlot/viewMaterial .htm?id=87158.

Peters, Gerhard and John T. Woolley. "Franklin D. Roosevelt: Radio Address on the 150th Anniversary of the Ratification of the Bill of Rights. December 15, 1941." The American Presidency Project. Accessed April 13, 2017. http://www.presidency.ucsb.edu/ws/?pid=16062.

———. "Harry S. Truman: Address at the National Archives Dedicating the New Shrine for the Declaration of Independence, the Constitution, and the Bill of Rights. December 15, 1952." The American Presidency Project. Accessed April 13, 2017. http://www.presidency.ucsb.edu /ws/?pid=14358.

Pritchett, C. Herman. *The American Constitution*. New York: McGraw-Hill, 1959.

Rakove, Jack N. *The Beginnings of National Politics: An Interpretive History of the Continental Congress*. New York: Knopf, 1979.

Ritz, Wilfred J. "From the Here of Jefferson's Handwritten Rough Draft of the Declaration of Independence to the There of the Printed Dunlap Broadside." *Pennsylvania Magazine of*

History and Biography 116, no. 4 (October 1992): 499–512.

———. "The Authentication of the Engrossed Declaration of Independence on July 4, 1776." *Law and History Review* 4, no. 1 (Spring 1986): 179–204.

Robertson, David Brian. *The Original Compromise: What the Constitutional Framers Were Really Thinking.* New York: Oxford University Press, 2013.

"The Bill of Rights: A Brief History." American Civil Liberties Union. Accessed April 4, 2017. https://www.aclu.org/other/bill-rights-brief-history.

"The Bill of Rights: A Transcription." National Archives and Records Administration. Accessed March 28, 2017. https://www.archives.gov/founding-docs/constitution-transcript.

"The Constitution of the United States: A Transcription." National Archives and Records Administration. Accessed March 28, 2017. https://www.archives.gov/founding-docs/constitution-transcript.

Thomas. "10 Amazing Facts About the US Constitution." *The Political Insider.* July 1, 2015. Accessed April 13, 2017. http://thepoliticalinsider.com/10-amazing-facts-about-the-us-constitution/.

Tsesis, Alexander. *For Liberty and Equality: The Life and Times of the Declaration of Independence,* New York: Oxford University Press, 2012.

Unger, Arthur. "Danny Kaye talks about his role in the complex drama 'Skokie'" *The Christian Science Monitor.* November 13, 1981. Accessed April 13, 2017. http://www.csmonitor.com/1981/1113/111300.html.

"United States (U.S.) Founding Fathers." Constitution Facts. Accessed April 4, 2017. https://www.constitutionfacts.com/us-founding-fathers/.

United States Department of State, *The Declaration of Independence, 1776,* 1911.

U.S. Bill of Rights." Constitution Facts. Accessed April 4, 2017. https://www.constitutionfacts.com/us-constitution-amendments/bill-of-rights/.

Wills, Garry. *Inventing America: Jefferson's Declaration of Independence.* Garden City, NY: Doubleday, 1978.

Wilson, Woodrow. *Constitutional Government in the United States.* New Orleans: Quid Pro Books, 2011.

Wood, Gordon. *The Creation of the American Republic, 1776–1787.* Chapel Hill: University of North Carolina Press, 1998.

"Writing the Declaration of Independence, 1776." EyeWitness to History (1999). Accessed April 04, 2017. www.eyewitnesstohistory.com/jefferson.htm.

WORTH BOOKS

SMART SUMMARIES

So much to read, so little time?

Explore summaries of bestselling fiction and essential nonfiction books on a variety of subjects, including business, history, science, lifestyle, and much more.

Visit the store at
www.ebookstore.worthbooks.com

MORE SMART SUMMARIES
FROM WORTH BOOKS

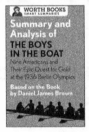

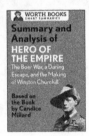

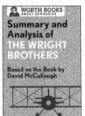

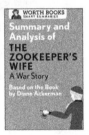

WORTH BOOKS
SMART SUMMARIES

OPEN ROAD
INTEGRATED MEDIA

Find a full list of our authors and
titles at www.openroadmedia.com

FOLLOW US
@OpenRoadMedia

CPSIA information can be obtained
at www.ICGtesting.com
Printed in the USA
BVHW08s1837170618
519272BV00002B/218/P